SAVING YOUR DIGITAL PAST, PRESENT, AND FUTURE

A *Step-by-Step Guide*

Vanessa Reyes

ROWMAN & LITTLEFIELD

Lanham • Boulder • New York • London

Published by Rowman & Littlefield
An imprint of The Rowman & Littlefield Publishing Group, Inc.
4501 Forbes Boulevard, Suite 200, Lanham, Maryland 20706
www.rowman.com

86-90 Paul Street, London EC2A 4NE

British Library Cataloguing in Publication Information Available

Library of Congress Cataloging-in-Publication Data
Name: Reyes, Vanessa, 1987–, author.
Title: Saving your digital past, present, and future : a step-by-step guide / Vanessa Reyes.
Description: Lanham : Rowman & Littlefield, [2020] | Includes bibliographical references and index. | Summary: "An engaging resource written for anyone interested in learning how to save their personal digital information. The digital era has reshaped the nature, scope, and use of personal information. This book analyzes the concepts associated with preserving and managing personal digital information"—Provided by publisher.
Identifiers: LCCN 2019051323 (print) | LCCN 2019051324 (ebook) | ISBN 9781538123805 (cloth) | ISBN 9781538171134 (paper) | ISBN 9781538123812 (epub)
Subjects: LCSH: Personal archives—Management. | Electronic records—Management. | Personal information management.
Classification: LCC CD977 .R49 2020 (print) | LCC CD977 (ebook) | DDC 070.5/797068—dc23
LC record available at https://lccn.loc.gov/2019051323
LC ebook record available at https://lccn.loc.gov/2019051324

For my husband, John Herridge, and daughter,
Lucy Marie Herridge.

CONTENTS

PREFACE

The digital era has reshaped the nature, scope, and use of personal information. People collect and store an ever-increasing volume of digital personal information on convenient portable devices and create substantial amounts of personal textual and visual digital information on their personal computers. Computer users have become accustomed to using a variety of tools that involve their interactive social activities. Because of social media, there is a large amount of user-generated content related to peoples' lives—and no way for creators to save it all. This phenomenon could result in a massive gap in our current history because invaluable information may be lost. So it is helpful to find out as much as possible about how to manage personal digital information.

Saving Our Digital Past, Present, and Future: A Step-by-Step Guide is an introduction to personal information management (PIM). It is intended for a general audience, and the book's premise is that everyone needs to manage their digital information. I'll introduce you to the kinds of tools people most commonly use today to manage their PIM, while considering the pros and cons of each. In addition, I'll provide visual and textual examples that illustrate how to use best practices to ensure the longevity of information, while considering current solutions to the problems associated with personal information loss.

This book begins by explaining what personal information management is and how to identify your personal information space and processes. Chapters 1 and 2 focus on the specific daily PIM processes, such as receiving, generating, keeping, using, and organizing personal digital information. Chapter 3 covers the importance of changing PIM behaviors to better understand why we acquire and accumulate personal information. It also includes a step-by-step approach on how to maintain out-of-date material and perform a "digital cleansing"—deleting all your unwanted personal digital information. Chapter 4 examines the problem of losing personal digital collections and discusses the many ways you can prevent accidentally deleting your information. It also examines the cost of managing personal information for the long term while addressing the challenges associated with losing it all. Chapter 5 highlights some do-it-yourself PIM tools of the future and compares newer systems to the traditional ones most people are accustomed to using. The chapter covers these tools and their unique functions and provides pointers about what to consider when shopping for digital cloud storage. Chapter 6 examines how to save it all and provides step-by-step techniques for the recovery and loss prevention of personal digital information. Finally, chapter 7 explores the future of personal digital collections and discusses how to maintain your personal digital life by creating a "digital estate plan." By doing this, you can avoid "digital foreclosure"—losing it all.

With my experience in the digital and archival technology fields, I have learned firsthand why it's important to save my personal information for the long term. I now get great satisfaction in sharing with others how to go through this process. I hope that this book guides you through this precious endeavor and helps answer your questions with regard to managing your personal digital life.

ACKNOWLEDGMENTS

This book draws from my own research in personal information management and was influenced by the everyday process of managing your digital life. The idea came from discussing my interest in this area with my dissertation advisor, mentor, and friend, Dean Michele V. Cloonan. Michele guided me through my doctoral research and allowed me to learn through her own experiences with research and publishing. I am thankful for her guidance, as it shaped my understanding of the field of preservation and how vital it is to maintain our personal digital lives. My editor at Rowman & Littlefield, Charles Harmon, helped me realize the utility of a book that addresses how we manage our personal digital lives by taking a step-by-step approach, and for this I am grateful. I learned so much in the process of gathering all the standards I have researched and taught my students about through the years. In my discussions with Charles, I gained a sense of how important it is to take the time to evaluate how we see our digital lives and what it is that we need to do to sustain them. Thus, this book was born.

A special thanks to Michelle Asakawa, to whom Charles introduced me. She has guided me on the writing process and taught me how to speak to the reader through text. Her gifted editorial skills allowed me to forego my more academic tone for one that can be understood by a general audience.

I could not have written this book without the support of my husband, John Herridge, who I thank profusely. On busy nights when I found myself grading my students' papers and writing this book, he was there for me—and for our daughter Lucy, who was about six months old when I started the writing process. He has been a wonderful cheerleader and supporter throughout. I want to also thank my parents, Iliana and Ricardo Reyes, who called me every day to ask how I was doing and to make sure I was doing nothing else but focusing on this book. I am grateful to them for teaching me the value of hard work and never giving up on my dreams.

Among the special people in my life who helped me fulfill this endeavor are the School of Library and Information Science at Simmons College, which supported my research and exploration in this area, and the University of South Florida iSchool, which allowed me to teach students from the perspective of these experiences. Last, I thank all of my colleagues and friends who have inspired me, in particular Dr. Gerry Benoit, Dr. Kristen Schuster, and my dear friend Miriam Kashem.

I

FROM PAST TO PRESENT

Contents

The digital era has reshaped the nature, scope, and use of personal information. People are collecting and storing an ever-increasing volume of digital personal information on convenient portable devices while creating copious amounts of personal textual and visual digital information on personal computers. Many have become accustomed to using a variety of tools that involve using interactive social activities on social media platforms. As a result, there is a large amount of user-generated content related to our lives and a limited number of ways to save it all. This phenomenon might result in a massive gap in history because invaluable information could be lost. Because there is so much to lose, it is important to find out as much as possible to save your personal digital information (PDI).

This book explores aspects of PDI to enhance the way you organize your digital life. Each chapter provides a step-by-step guide that shows you ways to manage your PDI, drawing from my experience as a researcher and professional. This easy-to-follow advice can be applied to your daily PIM activities and furthermore is intended to serve as a resource that can be revisited and shared with others interested in saving their personal digital lives.

1.1 A CALL TO ACTION

When it comes to your personal digital collections (photos, documents, movies, or music), you may find that you have a unique way of storing everything. At some point you may have your own organization scheme that works for you, and then realize that at times this organization may stop being functional. When this happens, you may learn that some-thing needs to be done and usually this decision comes too late. The decision-making process that usually triggers the need for a change is often connected to the worst-case scenario, which is unfortunately in-formation loss. To avoid losing it all, you can act before it is too late. Especially in our quickly changing digital world, where you may over-look changing your own methods and ways in which you keep your PDI.

The time is now to improve the organization of your PDI. Consider this a call to action, as it is critical to make sure the longevity of your personal digital life is secured. In the beginning the process may seem hard to carry out, but I assure you with my guidance you will consider this process as simple. This book will help you create a system that works for you and will teach you ways in which to manage and preserve your personal digital life.

1.2 WHAT IS PERSONAL INFORMATION MANAGEMENT (PIM)?

Personal information management relates to the organization of infor-mation and content assembled from private activities that involve your personal lives as well as the external communities you belong to. The phrase *personal information management* was shortened to *PIM* in the

1980s, and I will use this acronym throughout the book. PIM is defined as the act of managing one's personal records. A bit about the term's origins: the 1980s was an era of development for various personal information management tools, such as software programs that managed appointments, to-do lists, and contact information. PIM was developed in this era, but it has antecedents that date back to the 1890s, when the act of saving one's personal information involved memory and remembering.

You will note that throughout this book, I make references to memory, as it plays a key role in the way personal information is organized. Using memory as an aspect of organization will help you better understand the basis of personal information management as you keep information in familiar and most-frequented places. Knowing where to find your personal information is the beginning of the process of saving it all. The most important personal information to manage is one's identity. It is important that you maintain your identification data because it authenticates you, and it can be dangerous if your authenticating information is accessed by others, particularly now in the digital world. Personal information is fragile and valuable because it is uniquely about you. For this reason, it is vulnerable.

To start saving your personal information, it is important to think about the types of personal information you have and where it is located; this is where you start to use your memory. By taking some time to remember where everything is, you can take the first step in managing your personal information. Now, as you are thinking about where your personal digital belongings are, visualize what is it you have and where you keep it. When attempting recollection, you may want to focus on repetition, which facilitates utilizing memories that make connections to objects or activities in our daily lives. To begin accounting for all your PDI, you may use table 1.1 to create an inventory of what you have and where it is located.

Filling out such a table will assist you in organizing your digital information by identifying what you have and showing where it is. Memory is a crucial factor of PIM as it allows you to remember what is

Table I.I.   **Personal Digital Information Inventory**

PDI Type	Location	How Many?
Photos	Computer hard drive	350
Videos	Digitally stored via cloud storage services, social media, or personal web page	200
Music	External portable digital storage (e.g., cell phone, USB, SD card)	1,000

needed for later use, and it is the reason you can recollect things. Sir Frederic Charles Bartlett, a British psychologist, came up with a principle that is useful when you are remembering where you keep your PDI. Bartlett's theory of remembering describes remembering as a "reconstructive" process based on the ways subjects change and distort experiences when reproducing them from memory.

Everyone's lives change, as do the places where they keep information. In your lifetime, you may move into a new home or switch jobs several times; over the same time, aging occurs with your having no concept of how much of your digital content is already lost. These changes and distortions are components of this theory, which involves one consciously trying to remember rather than deliberately inventing material to fill gaps within one's memories. Now that you have created a list of your personal digital belongings, you can shift your focus to identifying your personal information space (PIS).

1.3 IDENTIFYING YOUR PERSONAL INFORMATION SPACE

The first step in the process of breaking down how you organize your PDI is to identify what your PIS is and how much of it you need to maintain. You do this by visualizing a space that contains all the personal digital information that you keep. An effective way to visualize your PIS is to imagine it as a rectangle. Everything within this rectangle is PDI that you keep and most frequently use or need to maintain for the long term.

Now that you have accounted for most of your personal information and have obtained an understanding of what PIM is, you can learn how to work within your personal information space (PIS). It is important to explore the ways you keep information that relates to you by establishing a connection to the space in which you create, manage, and share your PDI. A PIS forms the foundation for all PIM activities, including storing personal information in computers, cell phones, drawers, boxes, and so on. PIS is defined as much by what people would like to do as by what they can currently do with their personal information.

You will notice that your PIS is constantly expanding and is not just composed of files that you created yourself but also information created by others that has been shared with you. For example, if you had a photo of your sister's dog on your phone, it becomes part of the information within your control, and it forms part of your PIS. A PIS can be found within an electronic device, which can be a mobile device, a desktop computer, or a physical space where all PIM tasks take place.

The PIS is also associated with meaningful activities such as using a computer or mobile device to open personal photos, opening a book that is on a bookshelf, and making a copy of something because they are all associated with using one's memory to create a PIS.

If you are experiencing difficulties in finding your PIS, you can break down what a PIS consists of. Whether you have just created a file or are revisiting a previously stored file, it is important to understand the basis for the continued use of a PIS and that it is located where it is most convenient for you. The ever-growing digital age has made it possible for PISs to be virtually anywhere. You figure out what your PIS is by imagining a fixed location; although a set area seems ideal, the space can be flexible to cater to your everyday personal information needs. These advancements no longer confine everyone to a wall and chair, although there are many who consider a PIS to be a specific location—in some cases a desk or space where most routine tasks take place. Now, you may take a moment to map out what your PIS is, using the diagram in figure 1.1 to narrow your parameters.

Identifying Your Personal Information Space

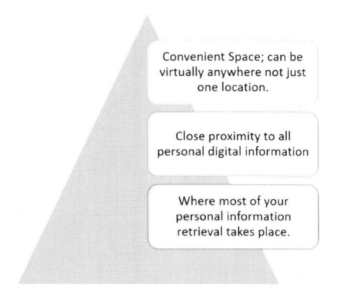

Convenient Space; can be virtually anywhere not just one location.

Close proximity to all personal digital information

Where most of your personal information retrieval takes place.

Figure 1.1.   Personal information space identification.

1.4 HOW DO YOU DO PIM?

The next step in organizing your personal information is to consider how to conduct PIM. Part of the PIM function is in understanding information and what you do with it. For example, you may have a system that you follow based on how you create, manage, and use your personal information. Furthermore, a PIM system is an information system that is developed by or created by you for personal use in a work or home environment. This system includes your methods and rules for acquiring the information that becomes part of your PIM system. By doing PIM daily, you are incorporating the methods and procedures by which you handle, categorize, and retrieve your personal information.

Now imagine a way to do PIM without a step-by-step system. You may want to consider creating file categories that allow you to place your personal digital belongings into groups. Your system defines how you carry out your PIM activities and should be personalized to fit your usage (see figure 1.2).

Visualizing your PIM systems may include reviewing your own digital files, photo collections, file hierarchies, notes, to-do lists, calendars, and contact managers. Your PIM systems are developed or created for your personal use or for work or leisure. To understand how you create and use your PIM systems, you must understand how it is done. This requires "performing it for oneself and dismembering it."

Using the PDI inventory provided in table 1.1, you can locate things within your personal information space, and you may narrow down where most of your personal digital information is. Making connections between you and your personal digital spaces will allow you to move on to the second category of the functions of PIM, which includes organizing and storing your personal information.

The third category includes the actions for later retrieval, where you start to place your digital information in places that are easy to remember so that you can make use of it later. The fourth category is maintenance of out-of-date information, and this is something you will work on as you organize your personal information. You may want to think about creating a schedule that will remind you that it is time to back up your personal files and consider what format your digital information is in to protect it from distortion and deletion.

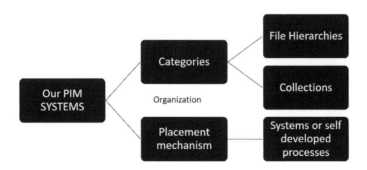

Figure 1.2. PIM systems.

The fifth category of PIM is deletion and retrieval. You have all your personal information in your PIS, and you either keep all things or you get rid of the unneeded. Having a plan for getting rid of your personal collections that are no longer necessary will help prevent overload.

Now that you have evaluated how you do PIM, divide your personal information into three separate activity groups as shown in figure 1.3. Visualizing this framework within your information space provides an easier understanding of how your information is processed, used, and kept. You may want to start by breaking down how you do PIM into three activity groups that represent the three support systems shown in Group 1 (those that support your information needs), Group 2 (those that demonstrate the need for keeping personal information), and Group 3 (which makes sense of your personal information and at the same time allows you to evaluate why it is that you are keeping your personal information).

Now that you have identified your PISs and begun breaking down your PIM system, you can focus on managing your PDI on one device at a time. This next step will focus on your personal computer. Many of the steps you will take for managing your personal digital collections in your computer can be used across all devices containing your personal digital files. Taking a closer look at your computer, you will see that you can store a substantial portion of your personal digital life on the hard drive. The average hard drive in a laptop computer ranges from 160 GB to 2 TB in capacity. Most systems will have between 500 GB and 1 TB

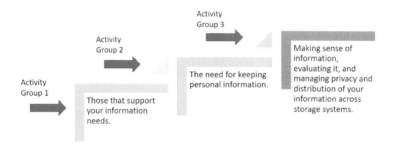

Figure 1.3.   PIM activities framework application.

of storage, which can hold over thirty thousand of your photos and songs.

Because there is so much room to store your personal digital files, your information can become difficult to keep track of. For this reason, it is important to develop an organization scheme not only on the desktop of your personal computer but also on your mobile devices and/or any portable electronic devices in which most of your PIM takes place. Doing this ensures the longevity of your digital files so that these files are not lost and are easily retrieved. In the next few steps, you will consider the organization of your files on your computer desktop as an example for demonstrating how to manage your personal digital files.

The first step in organizing the desktop is to create a design that works for your existing folder structure. Figure 1.4 is an example of my own folder structure. As you can see, I have created subject files with names that easily identify the contents of those folders. Many people do not think folders are necessary and decide that keeping files by categories may work for them, while others will work toward creating folders. The folders you create should consist of main folders and subfolders that can be tailored to the types of PDI that you keep.

Most of the challenging work in maintaining your PIS is in keeping a file organization scheme that works. You may have many categories, and your personal information may fit into more than one spot. Maintaining a consistent location for one type of record facilitates locating your information. You can then become more specific within a broader category; for example, within a subfolder of medical records, you can further break down the types of medical records you are keeping and whom they concern. Maintaining content-specific file names is an effective way to remember what is in your folders (see figure 1.5).

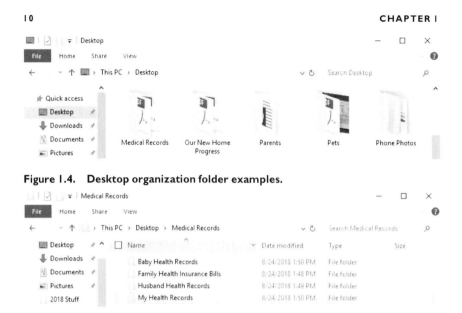

Figure 1.4.   Desktop organization folder examples.

Figure 1.5.   Desktop organization folder content, subcategory examples.

If you choose not to create desktop folders and simply want to have your files available throughout your desktop, as shown in the examples below, you may want to consider chronological organization. Chronologically organizing your individual files may be useful in your decision on the style that works well for organizing your files, and it can be accomplished by using a sorting command on your desktop. Note the following examples of different types of PISs that contain different organization schemes involving individual files.

Types of Personal Information Spaces

Personal information spaces include:

- A desktop organization scheme that is similar to a word document's right-justify option. This is where all the files are aligned at the right of the computer desktop screen (see figure 1.6).
- A desktop organization scheme that is similar to a word document's left-justify option. This is where all the files are aligned at the left of the computer desktop screen (see figure 1.7).

- A desktop organization scheme that is like the "parting of the seas." The files in this example are evenly distributed on both sides of the desktop screen (see figure 1.8).
- A desktop organization scheme that doesn't have any visible files (see figure 1.9). You may opt to hide your files on your personal device by using a hiding option within your user settings. This enables you to keep your file organization structure private when you are using your personal computer in a public setting. When you choose this option, your files may be found in folder hierarchies within your computer's storage drive. You will need to be sure to create a folder that will allow you to access these files without difficulty. This can be done by creating a new folder within in your computer's hard drive settings.

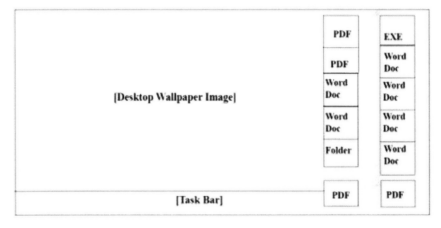

Figure 1.6.   Right-justified desktop organization.

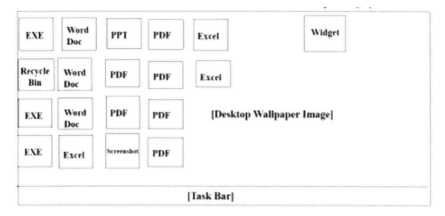

Figure 1.7.   Left-justified desktop organization.

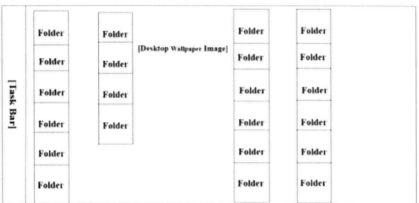

Figure 1.8.   "Parting of the seas" desktop organization.

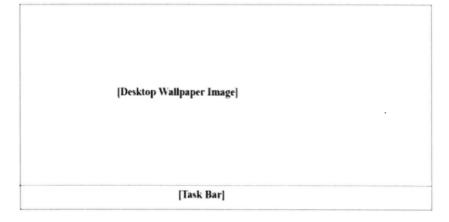

Figure 1.9.   "Hidden agenda" desktop organization.

Other people may use additional methods to categorize their PDI; there are far more methods than the ones mentioned above that can be applied. One significant factor to keep in mind is that while creating a plan for managing your personal collection, make certain to create a hierarchy that works for you and for the type of PDI you keep.

In the next chapter, you will learn how to break down your PIM processes. This will be accomplished through my introduction of the various components of PIM, consisting of seven PIM actions carried out daily. To prepare for the next section, you will need to understand the steps needed to carry out the following PIM actions:

1. Receiving personal information
2. Generating personal information
3. Keeping personal information
4. Using personal information
5. Organizing personal information
6. Re-finding personal information
7. Sharing personal information

Once you have understood the steps, you will be able to break down each one and further understand how they form your personal information management methods. You will be shown best practices as well as a thorough introduction to dos and don'ts.

2

PIM PROCESSES

Contents

When you organize your personal information, you are in control. When you integrate the information into your life by creating methods that allow you to manage your personal information, you are engaging in personal information management (PIM) functions—such as creating, sharing, organizing, and retrieving. Carrying out these functions is essential in understanding how people manage their information. In this chapter, you will learn how to break down your PIM processes. This will be accomplished through my introduction of the seven PIM actions that are carried out daily: receiving, generating, keeping, using, organizing, re-finding, and sharing.

As you organize your personal digital information (PDI), take a moment to observe the various steps that you will take. You can begin this process by imagining that you are making a list of the tasks that you need to complete. Doing this allows you to realize that you have been keeping, using, organizing, re-finding, and sharing your information all along.

So, how do you make sense of all of this? You start by breaking down the primary processes of how you do PIM, beginning with how you acquire and create your personal information. The objectives of these next few steps are to help you identify which personal information you receive versus which you generate. Being aware of these two types of personal information will help you understand the remainder of the PIM processes.

2.1 RECEIVING

The first step in the PIM process is acquisition or receiving. Once you have received a piece of digital information, you will work through two categories of activities: first, defining, labeling, and grouping; and second, organizing and storing. When you receive your PDI from an outside source, it is customary practice to integrate this information with your own personal information. Keep in mind that you alone do not create your PDI—other people can also create digital information about you. For example, an email you receive may contain photos, music, and content-specific files. You may also receive personal information through cloud-sharing services that enable you to share content directly from your personal computer or anywhere else you are able to store digital content. For example, your mobile device has stored contacts, photos, emails, and music. In knowing how to organize this content, you will learn about the different kinds of PDI that you have.

Figure 2.1 shows a close-up of my email correspondence with a colleague from work. Our correspondence indicates that we have been collaborating on several projects for which we share many files that span several file formats. The image shows the email subject lines along with a preview of our project file attachments consisting of various file types that coincide with the content. This example illustrates one form of digital information received from another person. When you orga-

Figure 2.1.   Receiving collaborative project file content via email.

nize your PDI, it is important that you know its origin and, in turn, its context and purpose.

If you are like me, that is, you have various emails with a vast amount of received PDI, you may sort your files according to content. Doing this should facilitate creating a file-naming standard for your PDI. This sorting process is important because it will allow you to dispose of files that are irrelevant, which, as such, often get misclassified. Taking the time to sort your received PDI *as it is shared with you* will facilitate consistent file organization.

2.2 GENERATING

When you create files on your computer, you are self-generating your PDI. In other words, you are the author of the content you are creating that is about you and relates to something you are a part of. This process starts with opening a software tool, such as Microsoft Word, or Pages on a Mac, that allows you to create content. I recommend that you save your files immediately after creating them, using a naming scheme that easily describes the content to you. (See sample file-naming schemes in section 2.3.)

Remember that naming your files does not need to involve a uniform pattern (though this is certainly helpful) but must make sense to you and allow you to easily identify the content of your files.

2.3 KEEPING

After you receive or generate your PDI, the next step is to establish a form of control, which you accomplish by carrying out *keeping* actions. When keeping, you must make sure that you understand what you are keeping while forming a system containing a standard as to how you access, handle, categorize, and retrieve your PDI.

The first task in establishing the keeping process is to create an organizational system of consistent file names as you look through the content you have already created. You begin by setting up your folder structure, which requires that you settle on a file-naming convention that works for you. The names that you give your folders and files should relate to the content in them.

For instance, you may want to create folders that keep the same file types together. If you are keeping digital photos that someone sent to you, you may want to put them in a folder named, for example, Family Reunion Photos or Photos of Grandma.

You may decide to use a chronological file structure, as shown in figure 2.2. My preferred format for date designations is YYYYMMDD or YYMMDD—for example, 20190514 or 191129, which are the equivalents of May 14, 2019, and November 29, 2019, respectively. This format ensures that all of your files stay in chronological order. Additionally, you can create subfolders for each year that you have photos for. You may find it useful to create a subfolder for each month of the year, or you may be interested in keeping your photos by year alone.

It is important to avoid long file names such as the one shown in figure 2.3, as some software does not allow file names that exceed eighteen characters. In this vein, it is important to also note that you can use a period to separate the base file name from the extension in the name of a directory or file—for example, 2018FamilyPhoto.jpg or

1920FamilyTree.docx. Alternatively, you can use an underscore (_) to separate the components of a path. The underscore divides the file name from the path to it, and one directory name from another directory name in a path. See figure 2.4 for an example of this.

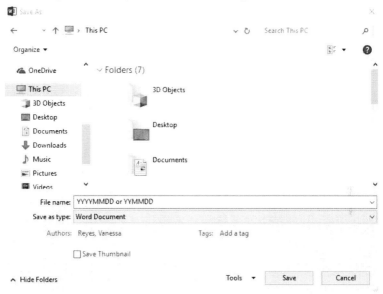

Figure 2.2.   Chronological file-naming example using YYYYMMDD or YYMMDD, to make sure all your files stay in chronological order.

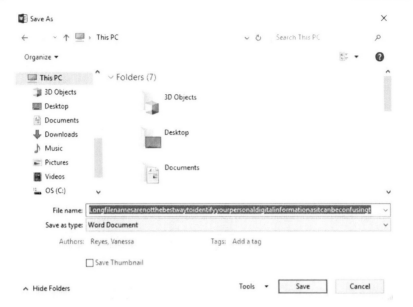

Figure 2.3.   Try to make file names short, since long ones do not work well with all types of software.

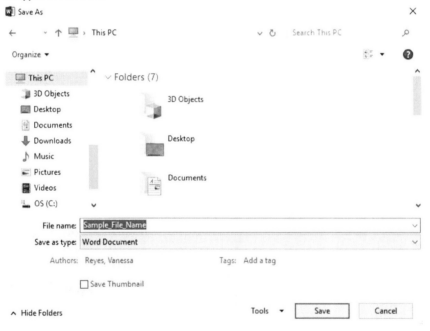

Figure 2.4.   Sample file name using underscores.

When you are creating your file names, never assume that they aren't case-sensitive. For example, although the names *BIRD*, *Bird*, and *bird* are the same, some file systems consider them to be different. I recommend you pay attention to case sensitivity, even if it is not necessary for most software tools.

2.4 USING

As a computer user, you have become accustomed to using a variety of tools that involve interactive social activities. Because of social media, there is a large amount of content related to your life that you have created, which you constantly use and revisit. Now, how is it that you use your PDI? Your PDI can be kept for later use, or it can be used the moment it is created. When you create information, you must make a decision about where to keep it so it can be found again. When you decide to use your PDI, remember the file names you create and where you keep them. Knowing the location of your PDI will allow you to retrieve it the moment you need it again. The process of keeping your PDI in a way that is easy to revisit is known as *organizing*, which is the next process that we will consider.

2.5 ORGANIZING

When organizing your PDI, make sure that you designate the appropriate content with the folder types that you create. You also want to make sure your folder systems contain consistent content names, ones that are thoughtful and easy to understand. While organizing, know that you are in control of your information and that you are not always going to need to immediately access all the information you create.

In fact, sometimes you might create new digital information without knowing whether you want to keep it at all. It is common to experience difficulties managing your PDI because of how easy such data is to produce—and to destroy. As a result, you may duplicate your effort in creating, copying, and saving your files. Just know that organizing your PDI is a process with many layers that you control. If you create the layers that you can easily follow, you will not have any difficulty with organization. The next chapter will examine in depth the methods you can apply to your PIM practices.

2.6 RE-FINDING

Your re-finding activities are driven by the need to keep your personal information, which involves making sense of, evaluating, and managing the privacy and distribution of your information. Re-finding your PDI should be easy if you followed the sample file-naming conventions that were provided in section 2.3. You may also use the search option on various devices (as seen in figures 2.5, 2.6, and 2.7), thus making it easier because of the reliance on searching rather than having to go through your entire hierarchical organization.

Figure 2.5.   Using the search option in email to search by using key words and phrases.

Figure 2.6.   Using the search option located on the taskbar of all computers.

In addition to searching for different words and phrases, you can use various operators, punctuation, and key words to narrow your search results. The most basic way to search is to simply type in a word or phrase. Figure 2.6 shows where on your computer screen you can in-itiate a search of your files. Once again, you can type in key words or phrases related to the file names that you created.

Figure 2.7.   Using the search option on a mobile phone to search by using key words or phrases related to the content you are looking for.

2.7 SHARING

An important part of personal information management is sharing the information one has collected, which is contingent on keeping and organizing decisions. Many of the choices you make about your personal information are related to how you will use it and share it. Yet, how do you decide that you want to share your PDI? First you must feel comfortable sharing it; you must trust the technology that you are using and also trust your PDI recipient. Do not share your personal digital files with others you do not know. If you believe that your identity has been compromised via email, your mobile device, and/or computer, contact the Federal Trade Commission (FTC) at IdentityTheft.gov.

In some cases, the files you want to share are about the person you are sharing them with, or perhaps you want to share a family photo or a favorite read. There are several different strategies for facilitating sharing. For example, you may choose to keep your documents in paper form in addition to electronic form, in case sharing the electronic form does not work. You must be very careful and deliberate about naming your files whenever you share them with others. Refer to the set of standards about file naming in section 2.3; one must choose a name that reflects the content that is being shared. Thus, your file names should describe the content and purpose precisely.

Now, a word about sharing your content within different storage types: if you occasionally back up your personal digital files using external hard drives, USB flash drives, and cloud storage software, it is important to use the same naming practices among all storage tools. Doing this will ensure ease of access to your PDI and maintain a standard among all your file names and will facilitate sharing.

Now that you have learned about the various PIM processes, you can begin to think about how many of these processes you are already using versus those that you just learned about. The next chapter is all about changing our PIM behavior—gaining insight into *acquiring* PDI as opposed to *accumulating* it. I will go over various methods of organizing and storing your PDI and show you how to maintain out-of-date information. At the end of the chapter, you will be able to decide whether there are items in your personal digital collections that should be disposed of.

3

CHANGING PIM BEHAVIORS

Contents

In this chapter, you will learn how to apply the PIM processes that you learned thus far. You will assess your PIM behaviors while going over various methods of organizing and storing your personal digital information. The purpose of this chapter is to show you the most effective way to organize your information by maintaining out-of-date information. At the end of this chapter, you will be able to decide whether there are items within your personal digital collections that you should dispose of.

3.1 ACQUIRING VS. ACCUMULATION

Part of the function of PIM is for you to understand information and what you do with it. In the previous chapter, you learned that the first step in the PIM process is acquisition or receiving. Once you have received a piece of digital information, you will work through two categories of activities: first, defining, labeling, and grouping; second, organizing and storing. Now, when you receive PDI from a source other than yourself, it is customary practice to integrate it with your own personal information. For example, an email you receive may contain photos, music, and content-specific files that you will upload and save.

The more files you get, the more you will add to your personal collection. This process is known as *accumulation*. When you accumulate PDI, it becomes part of your personal collection. You may also carry out the actions of accumulation when you are doing PIM. Accumulation consists of incorporating the methods that involve categorizing and then retrieving your personal information on a daily basis.

Now let's take a closer look at some examples of what accumulation looks like. Figure 3.1 is an image of my file folders within my external hard drive. An external hard drive is a computing device that stores information outside of your computer. As figure 3.1 shows, I have kept files since 2012 on this storage device. Accumulation happens over time, not all at once. In the past few years, I have accumulated my personal information and categorized it according to the time period I created it in.

If you are unsure of where to organize the various types of PDI that you keep, you may always use the preset content-type folders that are on your computer. You will find these preset folders in your computer's

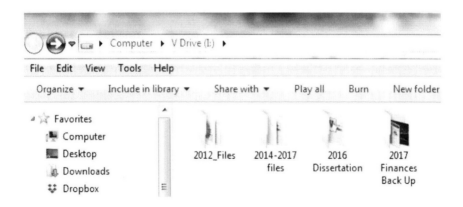

Figure 3.1.   Example of accumulated files from the past six years found in my external hard drive.

folder library. This is an option you can search for within your computer's storage settings. Figure 3.2 shows an image of my folder library. You will notice that you can categorize your PDI by content type whether you have documents, music, videos, or pictures; you can always count on using these folder categories to store your files.

As shown in Figure 3.2, you can arrange your files and folders into these various content folder categories. These are particularly helpful if you have difficulty deciding how to classify your PDI. One thing to be aware of is that these folders will also contain files that your computer programs automatically create and back up your data to. For example, let's imagine that you want to organize your music; you may also access music files that have been automatically created by software programs that you use. As figure 3.3 shows, my iTunes music software has created a folder. If we take a look inside that folder, we will see various subfolders containing specific data related to my music. Figure 3.4 shows what is inside my iTunes music folder.

Figure 3.2.   Preset folder libraries.

Figure 3.3.   Music library folder.

Figure 3.4. Music library subfolder contents.

This particular iTunes software, like a lot of other software, generates various folder categories that hold content related to music, including album artwork, media files that may accompany iTunes music, and even backup folders that contain copies of previous music library playlists. However you chose to organize your PDI, these are helpful places to consider.

Now that you have a plan for where to put your PDI, let's discuss the different organization and storage methods that you can apply to your PIM skills.

3.2 ORGANIZATION AND STORAGE METHODS

It's not difficult to create vast quantities of PDI on your personal electronic devices, but as new PIM tools emerge, there is an increasing chance that as you are creating your personal information, you are quickly going to lose it. Whether you have Word documents, spreadsheets, or content on social media, you can easily become accustomed to using various tools that incorporate all of your interactive and social activities. However you decide to organize your personal information, it will affect your life.

The organization process starts the moment you create your personal information. During this process you may share it as well as use it to help create new content. As you revisit these PIM processes, you are using various information storage methods, such as your computer desktop, mobile phone hard drive, and email storage space. Aside from these typical storage places, you may also be using cloud storage technologies—for example, Dropbox or Google Drive. Cloud storage technologies are convenient and offer an abundance of storage space online outside of your personal electronic device. The space may be free or at a minimal cost, depending on the services that you choose and the amount of space that you wish to have. In chapter 5, you will be introduced to various storage solutions such as these; for now we will focus on the storage process.

As you consider different ways to organize your personal information, know that there are a lot of organization and storage methods you can adopt. Storage methods most commonly used to manage PDI are:

- Save PDI to new folders on computer hard drive.
- Save PDI in computer content-specific folders (i.e., folders that you label according to the content you created).
- Save PDI to computer in My Documents (preloaded) section.
- Save PDI to computer in file folders according to categorized topic and name.
- Save PDI to file folders for individual files and for specific categories on computer.
- Save PDI by using names related to projects, document types, or assignments.
- Save PDI to desktop, then create file folders according to content-specific file types.
- Save PDI files to desktop and external hard drive.
- Upload your PDI to Google Drive, desktop folders, or external drive as PDI backup options.

No matter which method or combination of storage methods you choose, I recommend a consistent approach; that is, be consistent with how and where you save your files. In addition, I strongly suggest you save them in more than one place. Doing this will allow you to have access to your PDI from multiple places. If you experience computer system failure, having your PDI backed up in various external locations will aid in preventing information loss. Following this tactic will also provide you with a foundation when deciding what to keep and what no longer is needed.

A great place to keep your most-frequented PDI is on the desktop of your personal computer or as a shortcut on your mobile device. Creating these easy-to-find access points will allow you to access information quickly and efficiently. However you wish to access your PDI, keep in mind that you want to keep it in multiple places at once. Doing this allows for access to your PDI from multiple places, which, in addition to being convenient, gives you peace of mind: if you cannot access your PDI from one place, you can always count on another.

3.3 ORGANIZATION FOR LATER RETRIEVAL: DELETING THE UNWANTED

The organization aspect of managing your PDI involves developing a strategy to control your data. Without organization, information just remains where it was created or last placed. Information organization facilitates the management of your personal information and provides an opportunity to easily retrieve it. To better understand the relationship between organization and retrieval for later use, you need to consider the value of your PDI and how much use you will get from your content.

You want to start with getting rid of PDI that you no longer need or have a purpose for. Starting the organization-for-later-retrieval process by cleaning up your old files is the best way to make room for what you will need to keep for the long term. This is where you begin to consider what you no longer need. Let's take a moment to visualize this example: you have tax files from various seasons, along with photographs from past birthdays you want to keep, but have no idea what to do with them. You should start by moving these files and photos into content-specific folders, such as Tax Returns 2015, My Finances, My Birthday Photos, and Medical Records. You also want to make sure to place these folders in a location that you do not revisit frequently, as you may access these types of files only once a year.

The way to sort your PDI for later use is to make a list of the files and folders that you often use as well as a list of files and folders that you access less often—for example, monthly or yearly. Table 3.1 is designed to help you make an inventory of these items to better assist you in deciding what it is that you need to store for later use.

Table 3.1. Sample PDI Storage Methods

File Name	File Types	What Do I Need It For?	How Often Do I Access This File? (Daily, Monthly, Yearly?)	Last Time of Use?
Example: My Birthday Photos	Photos	Memories	Yearly	March 2018
Example: Income Tax Files	Word documents, spreadsheets, and PDF statements	Financial record keeping	Yearly	January 2018
Example: Work Files	Word documents, spreadsheets, PDF documents, PowerPoint slides, Audio lecture files, video lecture files	Work	Daily	October 2018

Creating this sorted list will allow you to identify files and folders you no longer need versus those that are most important to you. Most importantly, it will allow you to determine which files you need immediate access to. Focusing on later retrieval, you want to make sure that if you do not have enough storage capacity in the device in which you keep these files, less-frequented content can be moved to other places, such an external hard drive or online via cloud storage.

However you wish to store your PDI, remember that retrieval occurs because of a need for information. Retrieval allows the continued use of your personal information. The PDI that you decide to keep for later retrieval should be kept separate from the PDI that you use on a day-to-day basis. Now, take some time to evaluate your files and come up with a plan for what you would like to save and what you want to delete. In the next chapter, you will learn different ways to deal with information loss along with ways to prevent it.

4

LOSS OF PERSONAL DIGITAL COLLECTIONS

Contents

As personal digital information becomes ever present, the risks associated with maintaining the data you create multiplies. Ensuring the longevity of digital information is easier said than done. The most familiar problems are those associated with media failure or deterioration and rapid changes in computer hardware and software that make older systems obsolete on a regular basis. These are just some of the problems you may encounter as you create and use your personal information. You may even accidentally delete things, which will prompt you to ask yourself "And now what do I do?" In the event that you lose it all, you have this chapter to help you learn different ways to deal with information loss along with ways to prevent it. Most importantly, you will learn cost-effective methods that will help you maintain your personal digital information for the long term.

4.1 ACCIDENTAL DELETION

When it comes to deleting your personal files, you can avoid losing personal information by keeping track of where it is. Even if you are fairly confident that you have control of the files that you want to keep, sometimes mistakes happen. Information loss is inevitable, and you may find that you no longer have what you need when it is too late. In many cases, there isn't a way to prevent this from happening. Most information loss happens when you are unaware or is caused by computer systems and hardware becoming obsolete. For this reason, it's extremely important to keep up with your computer's software updates. Doing this will promote the longevity of your PDI.

How do you know your computer needs an update? Most computers will notify you that your software is out of date at startup or even when performing tasks. Your computer will prompt you with the steps to take to run updates. Allowing your computer to run updates will prolong the longevity of your computer system. If your hardware needs upgrading due to the age of your computer or because you may not have enough storage space, you should consider having your computer system upgraded before you end up with system failure.

One cost-effective way to check whether your computer needs repair or upgrading is by running preliminary diagnostic tests that are preinstalled on your computer's hard drive. These types of tools serve as helpful companions throughout the life of your computer. You can access your computer's diagnostic tools by running a search for a system diagnostic tool in your computer's global search. I conducted a search on my own computer for the word *diagnostic*; the results are shown in figure 4.1. You will notice that there are various choices resulting from this search. One of the diagnostic tests that can be run reviews my computer's memory, or "random access memory" (RAM). RAM is an essential core of every computer. With the right amount of RAM on your computer, the performance of your PC and its ability to support various types of software is optimized. You always want to make sure your diagnostic-test results reflect that your computer is working adequately. If there are errors found, sometimes your PC diagnostic soft-

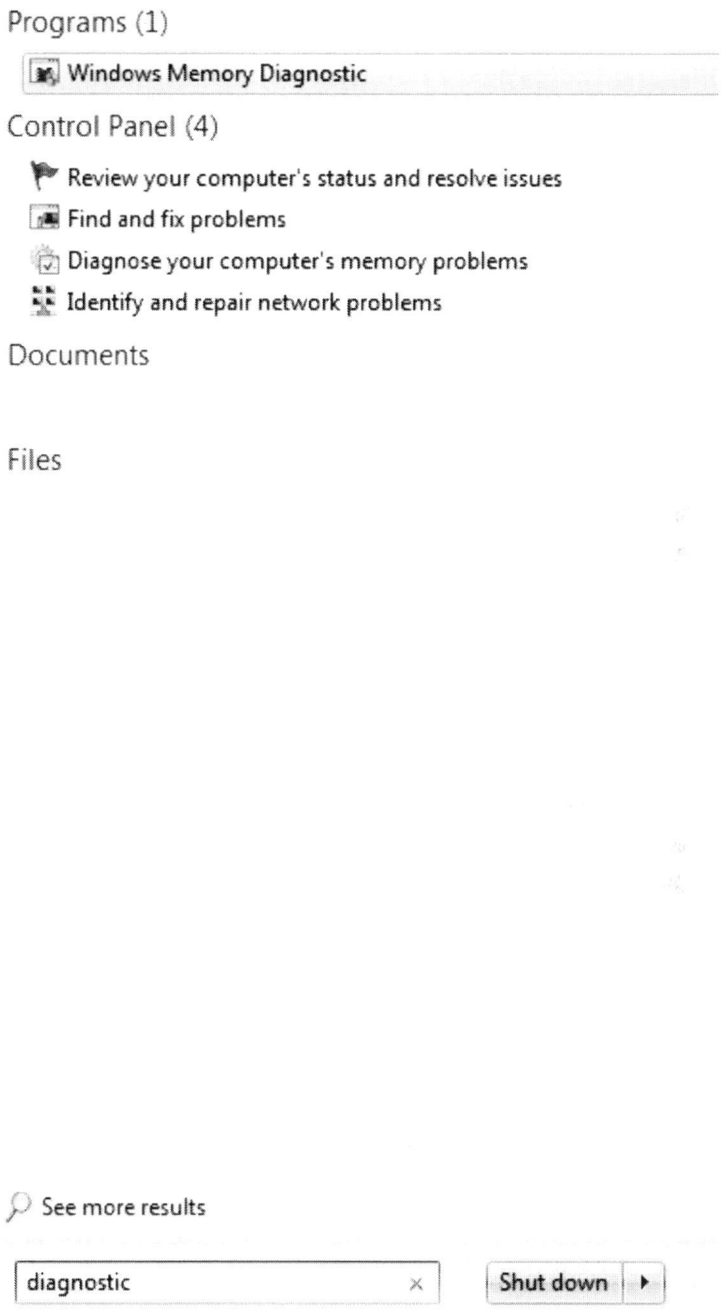

Programs (1)

Windows Memory Diagnostic

Control Panel (4)

Review your computer's status and resolve issues

Find and fix problems

Diagnose your computer's memory problems

Identify and repair network problems

Documents

Files

See more results

| diagnostic | × | | Shut down | ▶ |

Figure 4.1. Running a computer diagnostic test search.

ware might offer to fix the issue by running updates or uninstalling and reinstalling certain components.

Whatever your results, you want to make sure that you read through all of the options carefully. If you are comfortable accepting the repairs the program is offering, do that. Sometimes accepting the offered repairs fixes the problem and sometimes it doesn't. If you are unsure, consult a computer repair professional.

Within your computer's control panels, you may also find the option to review your computer's health status; doing so will give you options that may resolve issues related to software. Depending on your situation, there are various options you can try.

As you can see in figure 4.1, my computer has a preprogrammed diagnostic tool that helps determine whether my computer needs repair. You can find this option on your computer as well. After running diagnostic testing, if you still cannot determine if your computer requires attention, and are unsure as to how to proceed, you may want to contact a professional to help you.

Now that you know how to test your computer for software/hardware malfunctions, let's discuss other ways you can experience information loss. One of the most common ways to lose your PDI is by human error—accidental deletion. For example, you may be selecting emails that you wish to delete, and you accidentally get rid of something important. In situations like these, you may not know that you are missing something until you are looking for it days or weeks later. To prevent accidental deletion, there are various steps you can take to secure your PDI. Let's begin with working on the files that you keep in your computer.

As you gather the files that you no longer want, think of the places that these files are kept in. Most of the time when files are no longer needed, deletion occurs immediately. Taking your time to delete one file at a time may seem time-consuming, but it is the best practice to prevent accidental deletion. If you are sure that you want to delete an entire folder containing various files, you can drag the folder into your computer's trash folder. Keep in mind that even after you move items to the trash folder, they will remain there for thirty days. This is a standard feature on every computer.

If you are uncertain about moving something to the trash folder just yet, you can create a folder to temporarily hold all of the files under consideration. Once you have decided that the folder contains everything you no longer need, you can drag the folder into your computer's trash folder. Doing this will allow you some time to consider the items that you wish to delete without a time limit, rather than moving them to your computer's trash folder.

Now that you have some pointers on how to prevent accidental deletion, let's talk about recovering files you have lost. Have you ever accidentally saved over a file that contained precious data? Not to worry! There are a few options you might try. Let's say you just saved some changes you made to a letter you wrote earlier today, and you now have a new version of the letter, which no longer contains the initial text. If you have overwritten a file, you can always open your file within the program that you created it in. For this particular example let's say you created the letter in Microsoft Word; within this program you can click the Info option found under the File menu (see figure 4.2) and then select the Manage Versions option. Most content-creating software will have this option available for you to access. Knowing how to use it will help you retrieve previously lost content.

After you have selected the Manage Versions option, you will see a list of previously stored file versions by date, which you can then open and recover. It's important to note that Windows and most operating systems will only store the most recent versions, so it is unlikely you can recover a version that is several months old. If you have lost a file version that is several months old, you may need to use file-recovery software. Please note that this method may not always work, but it is worth trying. There's no need to be concerned about the cost of using recovery software as a variety of free and retail versions can be downloaded. Refer to the appendix for a list of PIM tools and resources.

The next step is to learn how to restore PDI that lives on the internet. Let's begin with your email. So, you have accidentally deleted

Figure 4.2.   Managing previous file versions.

email correspondence and now need to retrieve it. The easiest fix is by retrieving a message that has just been deleted. Imagine that all of your deleted emails go somewhere after you click Delete. Once you delete an email, it will automatically be placed in a trash folder, just like on your computer; you can visit your email's trash folder and retrieve messages as long as it is within thirty days. After thirty days, your emails will be permanently deleted.

If you want to retrieve an email that has been permanently deleted from your trash, you may still be able to restore it. This option may only be available from email providers that allow access to trash backup options. Usually the trash backup options are only available for one week, but the length of time depends on your email provider.

Let's now consider how you can retrieve accidentally deleted files from your mobile device. Your recovery options depend on your cellular phone's operating system; however, all smart phones allow the user to connect the phone to a computer via a USB port. Connecting your mobile device provides the option to transfer data from your mobile phone to your computer, and vice versa. If you cannot retrieve a file from your mobile device, you might try to transfer the file to your computer. In addition, your phone may offer ways to retrieve any file that no longer appears in your phone's drive. Some smart phones contain special software capabilities that will allow you to recover deleted files from your phone's internal memory.

In most cases, you would be required to install and run a phone memory recovery plug-in on your computer to assist in this process. Your phone will oftentimes alert you that this is an option you can complete once you pair your device with your personal computer.

Now that you have learned how to prevent information loss on personal electronic devices, let's discuss managing your personal identity.

4.2 PERSONAL IDENTITY MANAGEMENT

The most important personal information to manage is your identity. Identification is a necessity; it is required for people alive or dead, but someone else manages it after we die. Identification authenticates a person, and it can be very dangerous if authenticating information is accessed by others, particularly now in the digital world, because information can be easily compromised and/or stolen. Personal identity management is the practice of managing one's multiple forms of identification, including credit cards, driver's licenses, passports, and library cards.

Protecting your online identity, and recognizing the ways you can protect it, is crucial to maintaining your personal digital life. Your identity is an asset to any social media service that you use. Your bank, credit cards, school, and even grocery store establish accounts that contain traces of your identity to cater to your overall experience. Knowing the right steps to take to save your identity from theft will ensure the longevity of your online digital life. It is important to know that most identity theft will occur online when you provide your personal information to the wrong person or entity. Taking the extra steps to reset your passwords, back up what you save online, and read the terms and conditions after you sign up for a service helps in the process of preventing identity loss.

Malicious websites can trick you into following inappropriate options such as revealing personal information about yourself in an effort to take over credit accounts, online banking, and even social media. Unsolicited emails such as spam try to convince you to submit your information to entities that want to acquire information about you. You should insist on secure browser sessions to ensure that your passwords and sensitive monetary transactions are protected.

Data compromise can occur, especially when your credit card details have been taken and sold on the online black market. The compromise of your password is a precursor to identity fraud the moment it happens. Let's begin with protecting your privacy on your computer. Knowing the kind of user information that is collected when you sign up for any online service, whether an email account, social media website, or even your own online banking account, is extremely important. For this reason, I urge you to carefully read the terms and conditions that you are agreeing to.

These terms identify the kinds of personal information that will be taken from your private accounts and used for marketing and consumer research, sometimes maliciously without your knowledge. It is important to note that the moment you share your information with anyone online, it is no longer private—and the worst part is that you may have no idea who has control of it. I am not trying to make you paranoid; I only want to create awareness that in our digital world you must be cautious and mindful of whom you share your PDI with.

4.3 THE COST OF MANAGING PERSONAL INFORMATION

Managing personal digital content doesn't have to be costly. Thus far you have learned how to prevent accidentally deleting your PDI as well as how to retrieve missing information. You then were introduced to ways in which you can keep your PDI secure by following some simple steps to help protect your digital identity. In this next section, you will discover different ways that you can store and maintain your PDI without having to spend a lot of money.

Your PDI doesn't consist of just your work and personal computer files but rather includes all of the complex and varied digital information that you and the entities you deal with generate. As a result, you may have vast quantities of data, and it is not all kept in the same place. Take a look at figure 4.3, which shows various USB flash drives that I own. Sometime between 2007 and 2012, I was given these drives, commonly known as "thumb drives," at conferences and events I attended. Sometimes I found myself purchasing one because of how convenient and cheap it was to acquire. I often thought, "What should I do with all of these tiny portable storage devices?" I decided to keep them in a drawer and have made sure to back up their contents every year. Flash drives last about ten years, but data loss can occur in seconds. The same goes for all external hard drives; however, they have an even shorter life span of three to five years.

With newer, more reliable ways of saving PDI, it has become obsolete to use portable external storage because cloud storage is now freely accessible. For example, anyone who signs up for a Google Drive account will get 15 gigabytes of free storage. In addition, all handheld mobile devices now require users to sign in to either a Google account or an Apple iTunes account in order to sync personal data such as music, contacts, photographs, and any digital content kept within the user's cloud storage account. Whether you end up using Google or iTunes, all cloud storage accounts offer between 5 and 15 gigabytes of storage free of cost. This is a great way to maintain access to all of your most commonly used data across all of your portable electronic devices. To view a cost analysis of using cloud storage versus external storage, refer to tables 4.1 and 4.2. Keep in mind that these costs are subject to change; occasionally there are promotions that lower the price, but prices likely will increase over time. There is also the internal storage of each of the devices you own. Depending on how much available hard drive space you decide to purchase, the average cell phone or tablet

Figure 4.3.   My USB flash drives from 2007–2012.

comes with 16 to 32 gigabytes of storage, which is equal to about 8,000 photos or over 3,000 songs,.

If you think your electronic device's internal storage is not large enough, and you don't want to go over your free cloud storage plan, you can purchase an electronic device that will allow you to upgrade the internal storage: a micro SD card. These devices have been around since the late 1990s and have since then been held in high regard as a dependable option for storage. An SD card has the ability to double a device's storage for a fraction of the cost of purchasing a monthly cloud storage plan. There are various brands to choose from, and they vary in storage ability and quality. Whichever option you settle on, always remember to keep a backup of all of your PDI in secure multiple storage types to avoid losing it all.

Table 4.1.   Cloud Storage Providers and Pricing per Unit

Cloud Storage Service	Avg. Price per GB	Plan Costs
OneDrive	$0.007	100 GB for $1.99/month, 200 GB for $3.99/month, 1 TB for $6.99/month
Dropbox	$0.01	1 TB for $9.99/month
Amazon Cloud Drive	Infinite	Unlimited photos for Prime members, 100 GB for $11.99 and 1 TB for $59.99, up to 30 TB for an additional $59.99 per TB/month

If you would rather not upgrade your storage options outside of your electronic device or within the cloud service that you are using, then consider the recommendations in the next section, where we will discuss how to save it all with helpful easy-to-follow tips to clean up your storage and make room for your PDI.

4.4 RUNNING OUT OF SPACE: AVOID LOSING IT ALL

If you have space constraints on your PC or portable electronic devices, you may want to consider the various options presented to you in this section. You can start by removing the items that take the most space—PDFs, photos, and videos. You may also want to consider emptying your trash. Word documents, PowerPoint slides, and any kind of form files don't take up much of your storage space. When storing photos and videos, consider whether they need to be saved in their original size. Keeping high-resolution files will take up a lot of space across all storage mediums, but you can easily change the size of your photos and videos to reduce the amount of storage space used. On your computer, you can change the resolution of your photos by going to File Open, then selecting an image from its location. Next, click Edit or Image from the toolbar and look for the Image Resize option, as shown in figure 4.4. In this example, I opened an image using basic photo gallery software preinstalled on my computer. Under the Edit menu, you are able to see the option to change the resolution quality of your photos.

Table 4.2.   External Storage and Pricing per Unit

Avg. Storage per Unit	Total Cost
I TB	$49.99
4 TB	$150.00
10TB	$200–$300.00

The smaller the percent resolution of your photos, the less space they will take up on your device or external storage space. It is important to note that the photo quality will be significantly affected as you select smaller/lower resolutions.

The term *resolution* refers to the amount of detail an image holds and is measured in pixels per inch. The higher the resolution, the more pixels per inch, and thus the better visual quality, your image will have. Some other points to keep in mind: image resolution has everything to do with printing your image, not how your images or photos look on your computer screen. The generally accepted image value is 300 pixels per inch. Once you have selected the image size you are comfortable with, make sure to save the file. This will overwrite the original unless you also change the file name.

When saving your documents, sheets, slides, forms, sites, or files across all storage types, consider whether there are media attached to the files that make them larger. Any photos and videos that are stored using a high-resolution size will take up more of your storage space. The larger your files, the better the quality and resolution, but please note that better quality files do take more storage space.

If you are worried about your storage being full, whether it is on your computer or a cloud drive, you can still take a few steps to make more room while keeping safe what you don't want to lose. Imagine that you have filled your PC's storage; at this point you won't be able to store anything new. For example, you won't be able to sync or upload new files. You can still create documents because they don't take up any storage space until you save them. Once you want to save your newly created files, you will have the option of saving them externally. To

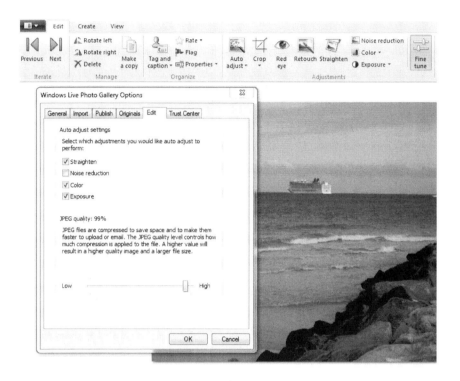

Figure 4.4.   How to change the resolution quality of your photos.

maintain your PDI and still have space for new things, you will need to learn the following tips.

You may want to periodically run a disk cleanup on your PC. Most computers come with a handful of great tools to help keep your computer's storage nice and tidy. The problem is, not everybody knows where to find these functions, or what to look for. The disk cleanup is the first of these tools you should use to delete data such as temporary files, which can amount to gigabytes of data over time. To access the disk cleanup function, first, go to your computer's Windows start menu, right-click on your hard drive, and select the Properties option. Under the general tab, click the Disk Cleanup option. Once you have done this, you will notice that the software will scan your drive and let you know how much space you can save by running the disk cleanup option.

Once you have completed this process, you may select the files that you wish to delete from the drive, and hit OK; just like that, you have removed unnecessary files that have been taking up space that you can now freely use.

The next step is to consider uninstalling programs that you no longer need or use. For many computer users, most of the disk space goes to applications and games. If you find that you no longer use certain programs, you can uninstall and remove them from your hard drive. Again, your computer will provide you with the ability to easily get rid of any unwanted programs. To uninstall/remove programs, first, go to your computer's Windows start menu and select the Control Panel option. From this menu you will be able to choose the Uninstall a Program option, as shown in figure 4.5. To easily determine which programs you no longer need, use the Sort the List of Programs option, which will list all of your programs by file size by clicking the Size header (found next to the Installed On menu option in figure 4.6).

Now that you can see which programs take up the most space on your computer, take a moment to decide what you would like to keep and what you would like to get rid of. To delete a program, you simply

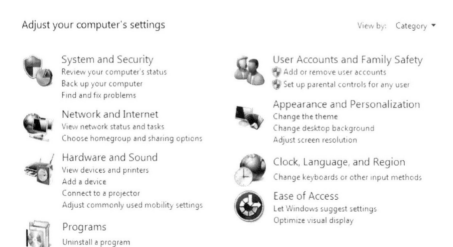

Figure 4.5.   Uninstall programs from a computer's control panel.

Figure 4.6. Uninstall programs from a computer menu showing "sort by" options.

click on the program that you wish to remove and choose the Uninstall option on the top bar. Depending on the program you wish to delete, it will walk you through the necessary steps to get rid of it.

Another step you may want to take requires you to carefully analyze your PDI and sort through any duplicate files you have. It is common to save files in multiple places and lose track of where all of the copies are. This would be a great opportunity to sort through your computer or storage drive to get rid of any of these files you do not need. While you are at it, you may want to also remove any temporary files on your computer. Temporary files are used to help recover lost data if the program or computer stops working. They also store internet history and files you may download directly from your web browsers. You will need to carefully sort through this list and make sure that you are not getting rid of something you may need for later use. To access your temporary files, first, click on Settings to open the settings window. Next, click on System; a new window will open. From the left pane of the new window, click on the eighth option from the top, Storage. In the right window pane you will see the storage drives that your system contains. To delete the temporary files on the drive of your PC, click on your Temporary Files folder. A new window will open up for the selected drive, which shows its storage usage. Here you can scroll down to the bottom of the window to find your temporary files to click on. The window for Temporary Files will open, and you will see a list of temporary files. Click on the Delete Temporary Files button in order to free this storage area, and you are done.

As I noted earlier, another simple way to free up storage space is to delete the contents of your trash bin. You'll recall that files remain in the trash for thirty days and then are deleted—but you can hit Delete Trash at any time to empty your bin.

After you have completed all of these steps, you may want to consider sorting through what you want to keep on your computer and what you want to store on an external storage drive or in the cloud. This could take a few days or even a few weeks, depending on how much PDI you have, but remember to take your time, as your PDI is precious and you want to save as much of it as you can. As long as you consider these steps, you will avoid losing it all while making ample room for new material to come in.

In the next chapter, you will be introduced to both old and new PIM tools that you can use to keep your PDI organized. In addition, you will be taught to use cloud storage to its full potential.

5

DIY PIM TOOLS OF THE FUTURE

Contents

5.1 INTRODUCTION TO PIM TOOLS

When organizing personal information, you integrate the information into your lives by creating methods that allow you to carry out PIM activities. This is possible thanks to several advances in the technologies of information management, particularly those that include tools for managing information—for example, application software that functions as a personal organizer, email, calendars, and personal wikis, all of which can be accessed from most personal computing devices. As new PIM tools emerge, people are increasingly creating new personal digital information with little worry about running out of storage space.

Whether for word documents, spreadsheets, or content on social media, you have become accustomed to using various tools that incorporate interactive and social activities. These technologies have changed the way you carry out PIM activities because PIM tools are now better facilitators for recording, tracking, and managing all types of personal information. However, not everyone knows how to use these tools to their full advantage. In this chapter, I will introduce the most commonly used PIM tools for keeping PDI organized and explain how to use cloud storage with multiple devices.

5.2 TOOLS AND THEIR FUNCTIONS

Which tools have you been using to save your personal digital information until now? To answer, start by evaluating your choice of PIM tools among all of your mobile devices. Doing this will help you better understand the evolution of the tools you use to manage your PDI, and you will gain a better understanding of which tools work best with your PIM style.

For most people, computer hard drives are the traditional place to store much of their PDI. Let's begin by determining whether you want to keep using your computer's traditional system tools to manage your PIM. It doesn't matter which operating system you use—Mac OS or Windows—as all personal computers come with PIM system tools that you can use to carry out your daily PIM organization. Most computers have these preinstalled PIM tools:

- email clients
- file managers
- note-taking software
- reference management software
- text editors
- word processors

Email clients are software applications that provide access to a calendar, task manager, and contact manager; allow note-taking and keeping a journal; and are enabled for web browsing. All of these are important when it comes to managing your personal digital correspondence and have been widely used since the mid-1990s. Email clients are used not just for creating emails but also for receiving and storing content through an archived system you can directly link your mail files to.

File managers allow the option to view, edit, copy, and delete the files on your computer and PIM storage devices. Your file management software has limited capabilities and is designed to manage individual or group files, such as software-specific documents and records. These types of file management systems have evolved over time to be compatible with the many advances in computer operating systems in the past twenty years.

As for *note-taking software*, I would call this tool a chameleon, as the capabilities of software programs have changed with the times. The first iterations of note-taking software consisted of the basic function of typing text that could be saved for later retrieval. Now you can multitask while using note-taking software; you do not need to commit to working in just one place. There are various note-taking software applications that can store your notes in the cloud and sync them across multiple devices. As long as you have the internet, you have your notes. Second, note-taking apps now have search functionality. In a matter of seconds, you can find any notes you need, even if they are years old. The best note-taking apps let you snap pictures and save them as notes, upload files, record audio, and clip pages from the web. You may be familiar with some of the most popular software names, such as Evernote, Microsoft OneNote, and Google Keep. See table 5.1 for a brief description of the most commonly used note-taking tools.

Reference management software isn't for everyone; it's a tool for academic materials, business presentations, and reports, which all benefit from adequately citing sources. These tools can be for one-time use, where users submit information and receive a full citation, or can act as a secure source repository for long-term projects. Reference management software can connect large teams through cloud servers, providing full-company access to trusted resources and articles. This was not possible decades ago, when the only way to manage one's references was by following a printed manual.

Table 5.1.   Note-Taking Tools

Evernote	An app for your smartphone, table, computer, even moleskin notebook that can be used with Android or iOS. It serves as your personal digital notetaker, PDA, pocket notebook, to-do list, etc.
Microsoft OneNote	A computer program for free-form information gathering and multiuser collaboration. It gathers users' notes, drawings, screen clippings, and audio commentaries. Notes can be shared with other OneNote users over the internet or a network.
Google Keep	A note-taking service developed by Google that is available on the web and via mobile apps for iOS and Android. It has a variety of tools for taking notes, including text, lists, images, and audio.
Simplenote	A note-taking application with markdown support. It can be accessed via both cross-platform apps and most web browsers.

Often, reference management tools can integrate with file storage and sharing or document creation tools. The difficult part of working with these tools is how they come together with the operating system being used as well as their functions and constraints. I mention this because it is difficult to provide a demonstration without showing how a specific reference management tool works on multiple interfaces, as well as the many options they offer. For example, using Endnote will not convert your in-text citation style to another citation styling format, but if you use Zotero reference management software, you will be able to convert documents from in-text citation styles to other citation styles. The commands may work differently, but the outcome is generic in that you will obtain assistance with appropriately citing your resources. Using this tool early on in the writing process will allow you to save your personalized resources as they're found in the moment instead of struggling to locate them later on.

Common features of reference management software include advanced searching, reference libraries, and version history, which, like your own internet history, you can save for later retrieval. Most citation software will allow you to create folders to store your resources by project or subject. This is where you can use your PIM methods to organize your citation folders for ease of access and use. Table 5.2 lists commonly used citation software tools you may want to try.

Text editors are tools for working with plain text. Technically speaking, words made up of keyboard characters are the only data in a file produced by a text editor. The text editor is a standard feature on all operating systems; Windows users will likely be familiar with Notepad, while Mac users are most familiar with TextEdit. A text editor may not be ideal if you intend to include any kind of formatting in your text, such as margins or specific fonts. You will be able to alter all of these elements using word processing software.

When you use a *word processing* tool, you are able to format a document for printing. Microsoft Word is the primary word processing tool for Windows users; Pages is the equivalent for Mac users.

Which of these types of PIM software do you most commonly use? Ask yourself if you want to keep using what your computer has or if there are other tools that cater to your PIM needs.

5.3 CONSIDERING DIGITAL STORAGE: EXPLORING THE DIGITAL CLOUD

In the previous section, we discussed various PIM tools and their functions; now let's consider storage options that do not involve saving things to your computer. Digital cloud storage services like Apple iCloud, Dropbox, Google Drive, and Microsoft OneDrive have one thing in common—they provide access to your files from any device

Table 5.2. Reference Management Tools

Zotero	A free and open-source reference management program to manage bibliographic data and related research materials.
RefWorks	A web-based commercial reference management software package.
Thomson Reuter EndNote	A commercial reference management program for managing bibliographies and references when writing essays and papers.
Mendeley	A plug-in for Microsoft Word (Windows and Mac) that allows you to quickly and easily insert styled citations. It automatically generates a bibliography using all the sources you've cited.

connected to the internet. This means you do not need to be at your home computer or even on your tablet.

You can access your PDI from any device that will allow you to log in and open your files. If you are looking into testing cloud services, know that most cloud storage providers offer free instant access to online cloud storage; consider this a free trial with no expiration. Amazon Drive, Apple iCloud, Box, Dropbox, Google Drive, and Microsoft One-Drive offer free (but limited) storage space to new users. See table 5.3 for details about how much free storage these cloud storage companies offer.

How do you know which storage company is right for you? The cloud storage service that will offer you the most up front is Google Drive. Upon registering for a Google Drive account you receive 15 GB of free cloud storage space without worry of expiration. Google Drive works particularly well with documents, allowing real-time collabora-tion and editing in plain text, spreadsheets, and presentations. Howev-er, Google Drive uses part of the storage space that you are allotted for your Google email (Gmail) inbox. For this reason, users of Drive need to keep their email inboxes under control so more storage space is available.

Windows users may want to try Microsoft OneDrive cloud storage, as this service will save all of Microsoft-based files in one place. As with Google Drive, OneDrive allows you to not only store your files but also edit and collaborate via Windows Office Online. However, this service only offers 5 GB of free cloud storage to most users (students with a university ID receive 1 TB). This service would be ideal if your job or school has adopted Microsoft OneDrive as the storage cloud for collab-oration. You would get the most space at no cost.

Every Amazon account is entitled to 5 GB of cloud storage. This is free, available cloud storage space for you to use. Unlike Google or Microsoft services, Amazon Drive doesn't allow you to edit documents beyond renaming them, so real-time collaboration is not an option. Amazon Drive only offers storage options and is most beneficial if you have large files, particularly photo files that take up a lot of space due to high resolution. Amazon offers free unlimited photo storage to members with an Amazon Prime account.

Having an Apple ID automatically gives you access to 5 GB of free iCloud storage, which can be accessed on your iPhone, iPad, and Mac computer or via the iCloud site from any device. Apple's iCloud will allow you to store documents, photos, and videos. Like Google Drive, Apple offers real-time collaboration across devices (see table 5.3).

As you are getting acquainted with the functionalities of cloud storage, it is important to know how to store your files in any drive so that you do not mishandle your PDI. You may be wondering how to get started using a cloud storage service. The first step is signing up for a service, but before you do, you should learn about the storage policies of each service. Any good cloud storage or backup service will offer a privacy policy that tells you:

- what information gets collected;
- how that information is going to be used; and
- whom your information is shared with.

Determining the right cloud service for you requires you to consider the kinds of content you would like to save/back up. For example, do you want to save your email? If so, you would ideally use a cloud service like Google Drive, which allows you to save email attachments. If you want to revisit a saved email attachment but do not want to go through your files one by one, you can conveniently search for them from the

Table 5.3.   Free Digital Cloud Storage Options

Amazon Drive	5 GB free and unlimited photo storage with Prime membership
Apple iCloud	5 GB free
Box	10 GB free
Dropbox	2 GB free plus up to 16 GB extra when you invite friends to share folders
Google Drive	15 GB free
Microsoft OneDrive	5 GB free (1 TB free for students)

search bar, assuming you have saved your email attachments to the drive.

Saving your voice memos stored on your cell phone is easy; all you have to do is back them up to your preferred cloud storage software. iPhone users, you can save your memos to your iCloud. First, open your voice memos on your iOS device. Next, select the track you would like to back up on your drive. Tap the Share button, and then tap the Messages option. You will then address the new iMessage to your iCloud address; finally, press Send. If you would like to retrieve your voice memos on your Mac from your iCloud storage, you will first need to choose the System Preferences option from the Apple menu. Then click on iCloud. Next go to iCloud Drive (make sure it's selected), click Options, and then select Voice Memos. While you are doing all of this, make sure that your voice memo options are turned on.

When using an Android OS, you can upload voice memos directly to your preferred cloud storage as well. All you need to do is open your Voice Memo application and tap on the memo. The next step is to tap the Share option. You will then choose your destination folder and select Save or Upload; you will be given the option of where to upload your memos to. Choose your cloud storage provider—in this case it may be an application such as Dropbox. Once you have uploaded your voice memos, you have completed the process.

Saving your photos from your mobile device's internal storage to your cloud storage requires a few steps. If you have an iPhone, first enable your iCloud Photo Library. You can do this by turning it on from your device: open up the Settings menu and tap on iCloud. Next, select the Photos option and select the option to turn on your iCloud Photo Library. If you have an Android device, you will want to open your gallery application. If you are using Google Photos, tap the photo you'd like to upload to Google Drive or tap and hold a photo and select multiple photos to upload. Once you have selected your photos, tap the Share icon and then tap Save to Drive. You may follow the same steps to upload your videos as well.

Music can take up a lot of space on your device; you may want to consider moving your albums to the cloud by following a few easy steps. If you have an iPhone, first load your iOS settings, then tap on your iCloud and be sure that you are in your Storage & Backup menu. Next, select the files you would like to back up, click on the Manage Storage option from the list, and choose your device. Last, under your backups options tap on Show Apps and select Music. To back up your music to your iCloud via your iCloud Music Library (where all of your music goes), start by making sure that your iCloud Music Library is turned on; this can be done from your application manager. Once you have done this, you will have access to all your music collections across all your Apple mobile devices sharing the same iCloud account. But this service only works for iOS and Mac OS device users who are subscribed to Apple Music.

Apple Music subscribers, you can also follow these steps to have your music added to your iCloud. First, make sure you are signed in to iCloud on all your devices using the same Apple ID (consistency is key). Go to your iPhone's Settings app, and click on the Music tab. Then tap on iCloud Music Library to turn it on. You may then choose to keep or erase the music on your device by clicking the Keep My Music or Delete option. Figure 5.1 shows the three steps needed to get from your Settings menu into Music and to the final option of turning on your iCloud Music Library.

Android phone users, you can store music on Google Drive. All you have to do is visit the Google Drive app and tap the button to upload files or folders. To upload music, choose Audio from the list of options. You can upload as many songs as space allows.

One way you can save time is by setting up your mobile device, either your tablet or phone, to back up all of your data (music, photos, contacts, etc.) to your cloud storage. You can do this by setting up a regular backup schedule of your entire device. If you have an Android device, you would do this from your Settings menu. Go to your device's settings app and into the General option. In the General option menu, select Backup, and select both "Back up my data" and "Automatic re-

Figure 5.1.   Turning on your iPhone's iCloud music library.

store." If these steps don't match your device's settings, try searching your settings for the app for "backup." Next, go back to your Settings and into your General option, then select the Auto-sync option, and finally select your Google account; your backup process is now in motion. Be sure that you select all of the option boxes listed to ensure that all available data is synced.

As you are backing up your iPhone with iCloud, you will first need to connect your device to a Wi-Fi network. Next, go to the Settings option and your name, then select the iCloud option and activate the iCloud Backup by swiping to the right, making sure it is green, and select the Back Up Now option found right below. Make sure that you are connected to your Wi-Fi network until the process is complete.

Similarly, if you have a Mac computer, you can back up your entire computer to your cloud storage service—this includes all of your files, such as your photos, documents, and music. First, go to your Mac's Apple menu, then to the System Preferences, and select iCloud. You will then be prompted to sign in with your Apple ID. Once you are signed in, select the iCloud Drive. On your Mac, you can find the files on your desktop and in your documents folder in Finder under iCloud.

To back up your personal information on your Windows PC to your cloud storage, for instance Google Drive, you will need to first install the Backup and Sync client on your computer. Then select the folders in your computer you'd like to back up. After you have completed this initial setup, your files will be uploaded to your Google Drive. Your computer can be set up to sync any time you make changes. Your Backup and Sync client will also create a folder on your computer named Google Drive; any files you put into this folder will automatically be uploaded to your Google Drive.

Having learned several ways to save your PDI to your own cloud storage, you are now more familiar with the various functionalities of your personal computer and mobile devices. The next chapter will cover ways in which you can prevent information loss. You will be provided with step-by-step techniques on how to recover missing files as well as how to prevent PDI loss from happening.

6

HOW DO WE SAVE IT ALL?
RESOURCES AND SOLUTIONS

Contents

This chapter covers ways to prevent information loss. You will be provided with step-by-step techniques on how to recover missing files as well as how to prevent personal digital information (PDI) loss from happening.

6.1 DIY SOLUTIONS

We live in a do-it-yourself (DIY) era. DIY refers to a movement of "makers," those creating or fixing things on their own without resorting to commercial purchases. This is the approach I want you to take throughout this section. As you are learning ways to save your information, you will be guided on how to do things yourself without the use of external resources such as personal information management (PIM) applications or software technology. Please know that there are limitations to using this method, but for the most part, the techniques that I will share with you will enable you to be self-reliant when it comes to protecting your PDI. The easiest way to start is by understanding simple solutions that can prevent information loss.

In the previous chapter, you were introduced to a variety of PIM tools and their functions. You conducted an evaluation of the tools that you use to save your personal digital information. Drawing from those results, let's think about these tools and how they aid in managing your PDI. Now think of ways you can limit the use of these tools by manually taking charge of your personal information's organization.

In this mindset, it is important to be prepared in case PIM tools are no longer supported and become obsolete. The first step is to create a plan to follow as a daily routine. You want to be proactive when it comes to saving your information, and the best way to do this is to make a list. Start by prioritizing the kinds of PDI you use most and the ones you often forget you have, as is shown in table 6.1.

Use table 6.1 to guide you through sorting your PDI so that you can determine which forms you most commonly use and which you hardly ever access. Whether emails, files, notes, reference materials, text/word documents, or multimedia files (consisting of photos, movies, recipes, travel itineraries, or music) are most often used, identifying their importance to you is a helpful and essential task. Next, ask yourself: Am I managing my information as a group or individually? This is significant because it will determine how quickly you will get through backing up your information daily. You also want to allot time in your schedule to

Table 6.1.   Prioritizing Your PDI

Type of PDI	Most Often Used	Why	Least Often Used	Why
Example: Word files Daily personal work docs	Access daily	They are my personal work files containing data to complete my daily duties.	n/a	n/a
Example: Family genealogy files	n/a	n/a	1–3 times a year	Access only when working on family-related research

perform these DIY tasks that will ensure the longevity of your PDI. These steps are illustrated in table 6.2.

The key to successfully saving your files is to create a routine that fits with your schedule—one that does not take away from your day-to-day functioning. Once you have established how frequently you are able to back up your PDI, you can begin following these steps to saving it all.

After you have created a list of your PDI files, go to your organization within your personal information space (PIS), that is, your own folder structures on your laptop, cell phone, external cloud storage, or even your Facebook timeline—whichever you use most often. Now, follow the fifteen important DIY steps mapped out in table 6.3 to back up your PDI.

6.2 PIM TOOLS AND RESOURCES YOU CAN USE

Now that you have learned some manual DIY methods for saving your PDI, make sure you are able to use PIM tools that facilitate your PDI organization. In chapter 5, I introduced basic PIM tools found in your computer, along with their various functions, particularly, tools for the two most widely used operating systems, Windows and Mac. In this chapter, I discuss tools that you can use if your operating system does not provide software that helps you manage your PDI.

If this is the case, the first thing you want to consider is a stand-alone backup program from a reputable software company. You will also want to consider backup software, specifically for file backup. This means you want a program that backs up any files you select. While some

Table 6.2. Steps to Prioritizing Saving Your PDI

Step 1	Determine which types of PDI are important to you and your daily functions.
Step 2	Take some time to decide which PDI is the most important and make notes of these files so that you may revisit them later on.
Step 3	Determine whether you are managing your information as a single entity or individually (i.e., by file type).
Step 4	Manage your time and create a schedule.

Table 6.3.   15 DIY Steps to PIM Organization

Step 1	Before you begin creating a daily backup routine, make sure you have decided where you will manually back up your files to. Determine whether you want to use an external hard drive, cloud storage, or your own device's hard drive to store your PDI.
Step 2	Be sure there is sufficient storage space for your files in the storage space you choose.
Step 3	It is a good idea to set up a local backup of your PDI as well as an external storage form. This is done by backing up your files to your computer's disk drive and, externally, via a portable hard drive unit. You may want to consider synchronized files between two or more devices; these could be your computer and your mobile device.
Step 4	Use the backup or sync tools that are included in your operating system, but remember that the key to doing things yourself is to skip using any tools. You do not always want to depend on system tools, especially since you are manually choosing the files for backup. You may take this step off your list, but keep this option handy as it is a convenient feature you may want to use but not depend on.
Step 5	Spending some time to customize your PDI backup will help create a straightforward system you can follow. Having a routine will be the key to the longevity of your PDI. Keep a planner that documents when and where you saved your most important files. Doing this daily will help keep you abreast of your files' conditions. Remember: files can become distorted or corrupt in just a moment's use.
Step 6	Always make copies. Choose your files and make copies of your most commonly used PDI. This can be done by selecting the files and choosing the option to make a copy of a group of files, or you can do this individually.
Step 7	Once you have created a copy of your files, you may move the copy onto the secure drive of your choice. For example, if you are moving your file copies onto an external hard drive, in any computer you can simply drag and drop your data into your external drive's folder.
Step 8	If you are using an online backup such as cloud services, follow the steps in chapter 5 on how to upload files into your cloud storage.
Step 9	Use versioning, a technique that involves creating a set of copies of your files as they change. This helps when you are saving multiple versions of your files. Doing this will allow you to retrieve your files from different points in time, without recent changes. While you are doing this, make sure to keep a list of the file versions and label them with file names that will help you identify your PDI with ease.
Step 10	If you are manually transferring your PDI content onto your backup source, be sure to keep your PDI clustered together depending on their content type and use. This is to avoid any confusion and misplacement of your PDI.
Step 11	Have a flexible criterion by which you select specific file types to back up (such as music, photos, and movies) as your device may only let you select specific file types to back up at one time.

Step 12   As you are working on saving your PDI on a regular basis, consider a schedule that you can follow related to the amount of content that you are backing up. As mentioned in step 5, doing this will allow you to allot time to complete these tasks.

Step 13   If your files are very big, consider file compression ("zipping files"). You can do this by using the file compression option on your computer. Doing this will help you conserve storage space and allow faster transfer of larger file sets onto backup locations, such as those found in online storage and on external hard drives; this will cut your file transfer time in half, especially when sending file content via email.

Step 14   The largest files are usually the ones that take up the most space. If you are unsure of how to prioritize what your most commonly used PDI is you can always start by saving your large files, which tend to be media files.

Step 15   Regardless of the way you envision saving your files for safety, manually taking the time to back up your PDI is an excellent way to preserve your files without the use of any file transfer technology.

programs will automatically select your most used files, be sure that you want to use your device's factory-set file types (for example, your photos folder, documents, music, etc.). If you are interested in backing up your files by only using image backup tools, the software you choose will have to perform byte-sized snapshots of your hard drive to be able to save it all. This means the software takes small copies of the data at a time in an effort to save it all.

If you are considering a full-system recovery file of your entire computer, which I recommend doing every week, most computers come with backup software containing a full recovery option for all of your files in case of a system failure. For this, any backup program should be able to create a recovery of your device's hard drive. Of the various program examples you can consider, take some time to research software that is compatible with your device's operating system, and make sure you are comfortable with the software policies.

Tables 6.4 and 6.5 list free backup tools, the first with software suggestions for Windows users and the second with those for Mac users.

Whether you have a Mac or a Windows operating system, there are many other free options for you to try in finding the right backup software for you. Keep in mind the aforementioned program functionalities and system requirements. These are important for optimum

Table 6.4. Free Windows Software

AOMEI Backupper	This software for Windows users creates full-system backups condensed into one file. It lets you encrypt and compress the backup, and it provides scheduling options to set up a time for the program to automatically perform backups.
Cobian Backup	This program allows Windows users to customize their file backups. It also has scheduling capabilities and lets you back up and save backups to numerous locations, as well as opening a program automatically before and after a backup.
EaseUs	This backup tool allows Windows users to conduct a full-system backup and secure backup files from any kind of malicious online attacks. It also lets you find your backed-up files easily by allowing you to tweak various settings for creating a full system file without having to use a recovery CD.
FileFort Backup	This allows Windows users to transfer computer files into a cloud storage service. It provides a helpful wizard that walks you through creating a backup, supports encryption, and allows you to define a backup by the file size or extension.

functionality. I suggest making a list of the capabilities you want in your backup software. What I have shared with you is only a small sample of all of the wonderful free resources that are out there to help you back up your PDI.

6.3 RECOVERY AND PREVENTION

When you are dealing with information loss, you don't want to hear that it is all lost for good. This section reviews important background information about the techniques associated with recovery and prevention. Keep in mind that lost files can often be recovered without any problems. Although you may believe otherwise, know that files are often accidentally deleted but are not necessarily lost forever. We tend to think that "delete" means that your information is erased for good. In reality, even if your information is missing (for example, you accidentally empty your computer's recycle bin), you have a chance to retrieve it. For instructions on how to retrieve the contents of your bin, see chapter 4.

Table 6.5. Free Mac Backup Software

Carbon Copy Cloner	Widely used to create full Mac OS backups and schedule routine backup tasks. It will also back up to any shared network that your Mac can mount on its desktop and performs a fast backup.
Code42	Formerly known as CrashPlan, this program for Mac users is an off-site backup program that uses the cloud for storage. However, a free version lets you create your own local cloud, so all your files are saved to their cloud services. Read more about this product's policy and what the free plan has to offer.
IDrive	This backup service is unique, as it can be used with both a Mac and a PC, as well as mobile devices. It provides a restore wizard feature that lets you restore files indefinitely.
Mac Backup Guru	A backup app that specializes in making replicas of your entire hard drive. If you were to lose everything, you would be able to start your computer again since the program creates a full-system file backup as well as the system program that starts your computer.
SuperDuper	This Mac software supports the traditional backup approaches— saving to a disk, an external hard drive, and even the cloud. It can also create a replica of your computer's startup drive in case you ever have a full-system failure and lets you conduct a one-step restore, which makes it easy to retrieve backed-up files.

Envisioning the file recovery process can be difficult at first, especially when you are dealing with your valuable PDI. During this process, it is important to know that there are two types of data loss: *logical* and *physical*. Logical losses involve the PDI that you have willingly deleted; physical loss happens when your computer malfunctions, causing the distortion and deletion of your PDI content.

Being able to recover your PDI begins with backing everything up and following a continual plan over time. You can restore your data not just from conventional hard drives—such as USB drives and digital storage cards—but also from other types of media. To increase the chances of your lost PDI being recovered, I strongly recommend you limit the use of the drive that contained them. The more you use this drive, the greater the chance that the space containing the file you need will be overwritten. It may be inconvenient, but remember that all data-recovery tools that actually work take time in analyzing the hard drive.

During this entire process of backing up your PDI, it is important to know that there are ways you can recover lost PDI as well as prevent information loss. Do not despair—data is recoverable, but this process often requires the assistance of IT professionals and costs time and resources you could be using elsewhere. In other cases, lost files and information cannot be recovered, making data-loss prevention even more crucial. You can minimize the chances of PDI loss by being aware of the risk of data loss and knowing how to prevent it.

Once again, the most effective way to prevent PDI loss is to *back up all of your files* and documents. Backing up your PDI means that you have at least one copy somewhere else (more are even better). Always make sure to store your PDI backup copies in different places to avoid loss due to theft or natural disaster. You may want to consider cloud storage, as it often has more space than a traditional server and does not risk crashing as a computerized operating system would. Cloud storage poses the least risk of your PDI being tampered with or stolen, but you can still accidentally delete it in the cloud. There is always the danger of overwriting your PDI files as well as their becoming accessible to hackers.

No matter how you choose to back up your PDI, make sure that you are conducting a proper backup before having major data loss. I encourage you to perform periodic tests of your backed-up PDI to ensure that your documents are accessible. You will want to have a schedule for maintenance that includes frequently visiting your files and cross-referencing content accessibility.

The next, and final, chapter covers the future of personal digital collections, culminating in a discussion of how you can maintain your digital life. You will also get a closer look at digital estate planning, involving the important choices you have to make legally and financially to avoid your own digital foreclosure.

7

MAINTAINING YOUR DIGITAL LIFE WHILE PLANNING YOUR DIGITAL ESTATE

Contents

In this final chapter, you will learn how to maintain your digital life while you are alive. We will look at digital estate planning, considering the important choices you have to make legally and financially to avoid your own "digital foreclosure."

7.1 MAINTAINING YOUR DIGITAL LIFE

When it comes to your personal digital information, you'll want to closely monitor it from the moment you create it. Doing this is not an easy task, as you create a variety of PDI in various digital formats in your everyday life. You also have to take into account the constantly changing nature of technology and social media. The tools that you depend on for saving PDI are constantly changing—and at times it is happening faster than you can keep up with.

Everyone has PDI generated through numerous smart devices, including mobile phones, tablets, computers, and even e-readers, all of which can connect to the internet. The voluminous amount of PDI produced daily becomes worrisome when you must rely on PDI stored online. Personal information management can easily become complicated when it no longer lives solely within your devices. Information in general is hard to control the moment it is online. As PIM technologies evolve, we are more inclined to store our files in various ways online, one of them being within the digital cloud.

As a result, we have no choice but to produce, acquire, share, and hold our lives and memories on a variety of digital media. This leads to personal information loss as our old records become lost or discarded in favor of newer formats or devices. This brings us to the purpose of this chapter: to address the concepts associated with personal information management and ways to maintain your personal digital life.

Effectively managing your own personal records involves a lot of planning. You will need time to sort through what you have and determine what you want to keep, whether photos, videos, documents, email messages, or other information you use to complete tasks. Using suggestions from earlier chapters, you created a list of what you have and where it is located. Now would be a great time to revisit your notes about where your personal digital files are. You will need this detailed knowledge when you prepare to create your digital estate plan. As you are revisiting your digital content, make sure that you consider what is really important to you. To help you classify what you want to keep, ask yourself the questions presented in table 7.1.

After you have determined which files you want to keep and are certain of where they are, you can begin to manage your digital life for the future. In the next section, you will prepare your files for your digital estate. The section will guide you in building your legacy and give you some insights on the role laws play in digital estate planning.

Table 7.1. Personal Digital Content Value Questionnaire

File Name	Question	Yes or No	Why Are They Important?	Where Are They Located?
Example: 2005_GradPics	Are these files important to me? Do they have a sentimental value? Would I like future generations of friends and family members to see this information? Are any of these files important legal documents that need to be kept for a period of time?	Example: Yes	Example: Family member's graduation photos/ memories	Example: Computer desktop folder labeled "Family_Events"; also in cell phone storage

7.2 DIGITAL ESTATE PLANNING

Just as you consider how to distribute physical belongings after death, you need to plan for your digital property: that is, your *digital estate.* People tend not to think about what will happen to their personal information when they die—certainly, past generations didn't the way we do in the twenty-first century—but it's becoming more and more important to devise a digital estate plan before a debilitating illness or death. Doing so will save your loved ones much effort and grief (for example, in trying to locate passwords) and will protect you from having PDI shared that you would rather keep from others.

Recall how you earlier created an inventory of your PDI; you can use those inventory templates to create a list of your most important information, identifying what this information is and where it is located. I recommend you be as thorough as possible, being sure to include all devices that contain your PDI. Table 7.2 lists the most common technology devices that house your PDI. Once you have identified all the devices containing your PDI, refer to table 7.3 for a sample checklist of your personal digital assets. Keep in mind that the more detailed you

are about the location of your information, the easier it will be for you
and your family to find.

Once you have accounted for your personal digital files, make sure
you provide your loved ones or designated digital-life custodian with the
location of your online accounts as well as access to all of the information they will need to retrieve your files. See the sample custodial information sheet in table 7.4 for an example of the content that you would
need to gather for your designated digital custodian.

Because passwords are private, in many instances, they can be given
to survivors only after a formal request has been processed in court. By
compiling your list of PDI passwords and other log-on information, you
will ensure that your family members can access your digital legacy
without having to ask websites, software applications, and social media—even computer companies such as Apple or Microsoft—for your
user sign-in details.

You will also want to determine whether your digital information has
any financial value. If it does, you will need to have it appraised.

Appraising your PDI involves measuring the value of your digital
content. This depends solely on the types of information you keep. You,
the owner of the files, must make an initial evaluation. You are the first
person who should judge whether your personal digital content is of
value. To help you through this process, refer to table 7.5. Use the
questions in this table to gain a better sense of the important role your
PDI plays in your everyday life.

Table 7.2. Location Inventory for Personal Digital Information Management Devices

Personal Digital Information Managers: Physical Technology Devices	Location
Personal computers: desktop, laptop, tablet	Example: in home office, on desk
Mobile phone	Example: with me at all times
Music player (e.g., iPod)	
E-reader	
Digital cameras	

Table 7.3. Digital Information Location Inventory

Personal Digital Information Types	Location
Social media: websites, portfolios, blogs, domains, intellectual property, trademarks	Example: web browser bookmarked folder contains websites, Word file on computer desktop drive contains a list of social media profiles with passwords and website access link information
	Financial: online credit card payment login information, online banking, PayPal, etc.
	Paid digital content: films, photos, e-books, music, etc.
	Passwords: all online social media, financial, paid content
	Personal digital photos (JPEG, PNGS)
	Word files (DOCs)
	Videos (MOV, MP4)

When you have finished judging the value of your PDI, decide whether any of your personal digital files should be saved and passed on to your family or outside organizations. If you are unsure whether your PDI has financial value, I suggest you consult a professional specializing in personal digital content valuation. This is not simple, as it will take some time for you and a professional to gather and evaluate why these materials are important and whether they can be sold or possess monetary value. There are companies that will do this for you and even manage your digital files during your life and after your life—but these services will come at a cost. If you are interested in contacting a professional, start by googling "digital asset appraisal," "media valuation services," or "intangible asset appraisals."

7.3 DESIGNATING YOUR DIGITAL ESTATE CUSTODIAN

A common problem from not having a digital estate plan is online identity theft. For this reason, make sure a stranger doesn't take charge of the fate of your PDI. Plan whom you will designate to manage your

Table 7.4.   Personal Digital Collection: Custodial Information Sheet

File Type	File Name	Location	Collection Goals	Person in Charge of Records
[examples]	Social media user names and passwords	External hard drive in closet; saved in a passwords folder found on computer's file drive	Share with children and grandkids	Husband is first in charge; if husband unavailable to access content then child is in charge

personal digital content; this person (or company) will distribute or safeguard your content after you die.

Whomever you choose (whether an individual or a company), make sure that they will carry out your wishes. With the help of an attorney, you can place a clause in your will documenting whom you have appointed to be your digital estate custodian as well as which portions of your digital estate are assigned to him or her. The challenging aspect of legally appointing someone to take charge of your digital estate is that the laws vary by U.S. state and all over the world and, unfortunately, the law has not yet caught up with digital estate planning. Inheritance laws exist only for physical property, and there is no guarantee that your personal digital life will stand the test of time. For this reason, there are various legal issues when it comes to a digital legacy.

Once you decide who your designated custodian will be, you will need to create a list of instructions for managing and preserving your personal digital files. Specifically, when you are dealing with online social media, you should consider how you want to be remembered online. Social media websites like Facebook, Twitter, and Instagram give the option of turning your page into a memorial. However, all social media sites offer different options for how content will show up after you die. For example, on Instagram, any posts the deceased person shared, including photos and videos, stay on Instagram and are visible to the audience they were shared with, but the page will not appear in public spaces, such as on their account registry and suggested pages to follow. Another caveat is that Instagram and various other

Table 7.5. Personal Digital Content Evaluation Checklist

Asset Name	Question	Answer
Write the file type/file name here that the questions in the next column are about.	Do these files interest me?	"yes" or "no" to the questions in the middle column of this table, then explain why this data informs part of your personal digital life.
	Do these files have emotional value?	
	Do these files have financial value?	
	Are these files important to my identity?	
	Do these files tell a story about my life?	
	Would my family want to keep these files as a memory of me?	
	Can the files be quickly accessed? Or do they require a user name and password for access?	

social media websites do not allow anyone to log onto a memorialized account. Once memorialized, no one will be able to make changes to any of the account's existing posts or information; this is done to preserve the user's page as it was when they were living.

On Facebook, you can choose to either appoint a legacy contact to look after your memorialized account or have the account permanently deleted. If you don't choose to have your account permanently deleted, Facebook will memorialize it if aware of your passing. As you plan on how you want your personal digital life preserved, consider searching through each website's memorialization or after-death instructions, as each site will offer different options.

7.4 THE FUTURE OF PERSONAL DIGITAL COLLECTIONS

I started this book by explaining that personal information management (PIM) consists of a group of activities carried out to create, manage, organize, and share personal digital records. You use PIM in part to determine whether to keep PDI for the long term. Although how you create and store personal digital records continues to change, you can agree that it is important to identify how records are kept and where they are stored.

When organizing and managing your PDI, you rely on the many digital storage opportunities freely available. Yes, we can now keep as much as we want—and there is certainly no problem with keeping it all—but the challenge lies in maintaining it. Specifically, when it comes to managing large quantities of digital information, you tend to not know the value of your personal digital files. For this reason, I introduced you to several ways to classify your PDI and gave you checklists, along with important questions to answer, that prompt you to decide which PDI you want to keep.

We considered the benefits and drawbacks of cloud storage—saving your files externally so that they can be retrieved on any device outside of your own computer's hard drive. When you use cloud services, your files are stored on a server that is managed by a third party. Often the third party has a privacy policy that states that the information being stored in the cloud will not be shared or disclosed with anyone other than the user who created the files. Getting well acquainted with storage policies and privacy are important, as you are entrusting a company to safeguard your personal digital life.

I introduced you to a variety of PIM behaviors while going over various organization methods for storing your PDI. This was to show you the most effective ways to organize your information by maintaining out-of-date files. Being able to maintain out-of-date data allows you to decide whether your personal information is durable and which of it should be disposed of.

I also introduced you to both old and new PIM tools that you can use to keep your PDI organized. In addition, I provided you with an in-depth view of the key storage functionalities of your personal computer and mobile devices and with step-by-step techniques on how to recover missing files, as well as how to prevent PDI loss.

Finally, I explained digital estate planning, with consideration of which forms of your PDI you would like to be made available after your death and whom to entrust with maintaining it. Managing your digital information doesn't have to be a difficult task. You now have the necessary tools along with a long list of options available to help you manage and preserve your personal digital files.

No matter how you choose to manage your PDI, you will want to have various options for ensuring the safety and security of your records. No matter which PIM you choose, I hope that your collections are now more accessible and that you have a better grasp of how to save them all.

APPENDIX

Resources

This appendix contains a full list of resources mentioned in this book, arranged by topic.

Digital Storage/Digital Cloud

Amazon Drive: www.amazon.com/drive
Apple iCloud: www.icloud.com
Box: www.box.com
Dropbox: www.dropbox.com
Google Drive: www.drive.google.com
Microsoft OneDrive: www.onedrive.live.com

Personal Organizers

EverNote: www.evernote.com
Google Keep: www.keep.google.com
Microsoft OneNote: www.onenote.com
Simplenote: www.simplenote.com

Citation Managers

Mendeley: www.mendeley.com
RefWorks: www.refworks.com
Zotero: www.zotero.org

Backup and Sync Services

AOMET Backupper: www.backup-utility.com
Backup Guru: www.backupguru.in
Carbon Copy Cloner: www.bombich.com
Cobian Backup: www.cobiansoft.com
Code42: www.code42.com
Ease US: www.easeus.com
FileFort: www.nchsoftware.com
IDrive: www.idrive.com
SuperDuper software: www.superduper.en.softonic.com

INDEX

ABOUT THE AUTHOR

Vanessa Reyes is an instructor in the School of Information at the University of South Florida. Prior to this she was an adjunct faculty member at the Simmons College School of Library & Information Science. She received her PhD in 2016 from Simmons SLIS and holds an MS in library and information studies from Florida State University. Reyes's work in public libraries, special collections, and archives inspired her to pursue research in preservation, digital libraries, and archives. She conducts research that analyzes personal digital collections to understand how they are created, managed, and made accessible. She is also interested in how students and professors use personal digital information. Her current research contributes to the emerging field of personal information management (PIM), quantifying how individual users are organizing, managing, and preserving digital information.